D0624152

Out of this WORLD

ICY COMETS

Sometimes Have Tails

by Chaya Glaser

Consultant: Karly M. Pitman, PhD
Planetary Science Institute
Tucson, Arizona

BEARPORT PUBLISHING

New York, New York

Credits
Cover, © ESA/Rosetta/MPS for OSIRIS Team MPS/UPD/LAM/IAA/SSO/INTA/UPM/DASP/IDA; TOC, © NASA; 4–5, © Damian Peach/Science Photo Library; 7, © ESA/Rosetta/MPS for OSIRIS Team MPS/UPD/LAM/IAA/SSO/INTA/UPM/DASP/IDA; 8–9, © Wikipedia & Nasa; 10–11, © E. Kolmhofer, H. Raab, Johannes-Kepler-Observatory, Linz, Austria/Wikipedia; 12–13, © Cassini Imaging Team, SSI, JPL, ESA, NASA; 14–15, © Michael Jäger & Gerald Rhemann; 16–17, © Detlev van Ravenswaay/Science Photo Library; 18, © Halley Multicolor Camera Team, Giotto Project, ESA; 19, © Ralf Hirschberger/dpa/Corbis; 20–21, © NASA; 23TL, © iStock/Thinkstock; 23TR, © Wikipedia & Nasa; 23BL, © Wikipedia & Nasa; 23BR, © NASA.

Publisher: Kenn Goin
Editor: Jessica Rudolph
Creative Director: Spencer Brinker
Design: Debrah Kaiser
Photo Researcher: Michael Win

Library of Congress Cataloging-in-Publication Data

Glaser, Chaya, author.
Icy comets : sometimes have tails / by Chaya Glaser.
pages cm. – (Out of this world)
Includes bibliographical references and index.
ISBN 978-1-62724-572-2 (library binding) – ISBN 1-62724-572-3 (library binding)
1. Comets–Juvenile literature. I. Title.
QB721.5.G53 2015
523.6–dc23

2014040708

Copyright © 2015 Bearport Publishing Company, Inc. All rights reserved. No part of this publication may be reproduced in whole or in part, stored in any retrieval system, or transmitted in any form or by any means, electronic, mechanical, photocopying, recording, or otherwise, without written permission from the publisher.

For more information, write to Bearport Publishing Company, Inc., 45 West 21st Street, Suite 3B, New York, New York 10010. Printed in the United States of America.

10 9 8 7 6 5 4 3 2 1

CONTENTS

Comets 4

Comets Versus Earth 22

Glossary 23

Index 24

Read More 24

Learn More Online 24

About the Author 24

What objects in space sometimes have tails?

COMETS!

Comet tail

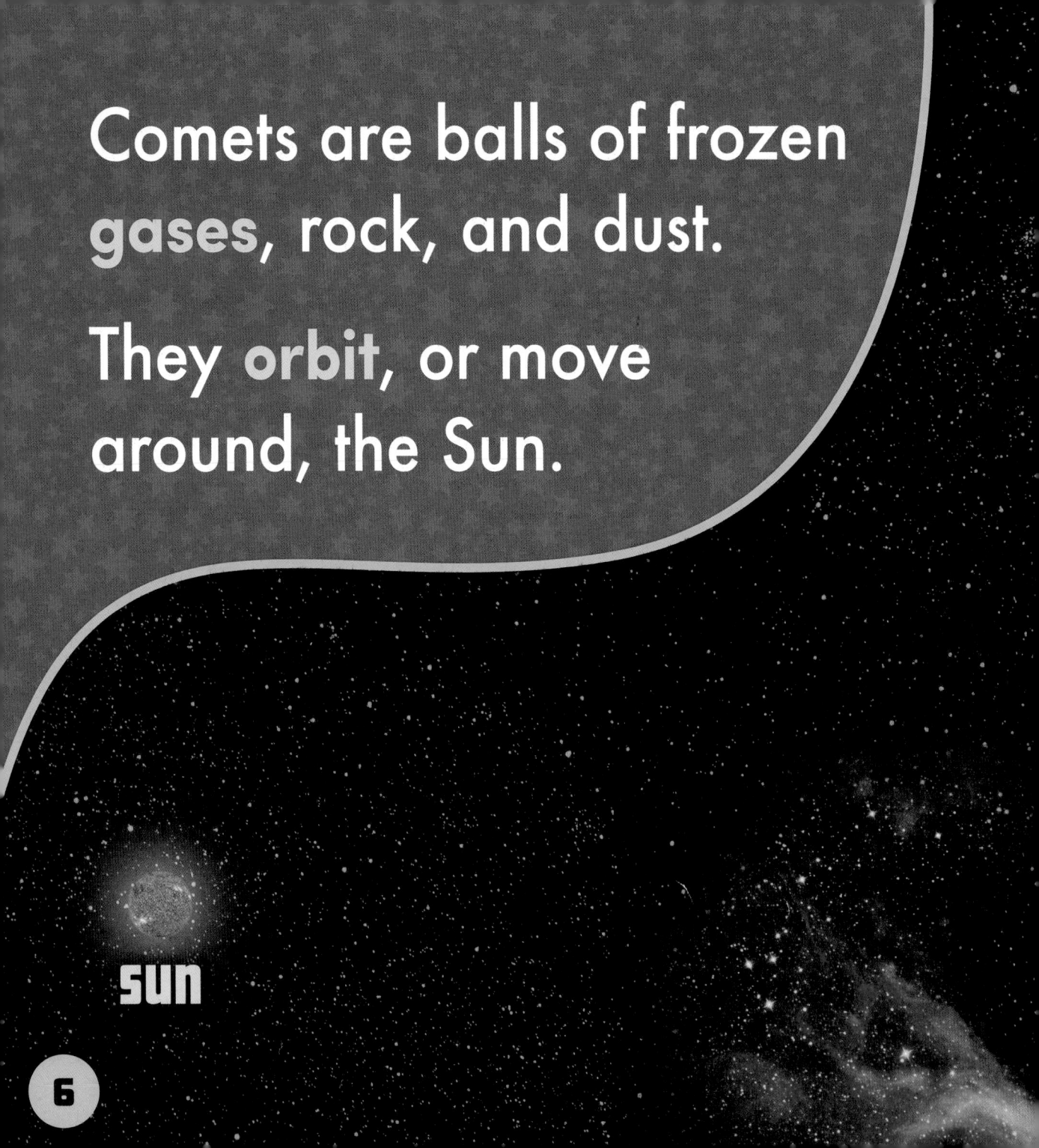

Comets are balls of frozen **gases**, rock, and dust.

They **orbit**, or move around, the Sun.

sun

Sometimes a comet is very far from the Sun.

It has no tails then.

Sometimes a comet is closer to the Sun.

The Sun's heat warms the comet.

The heat makes the comet give off gas and bits of rock or dust.

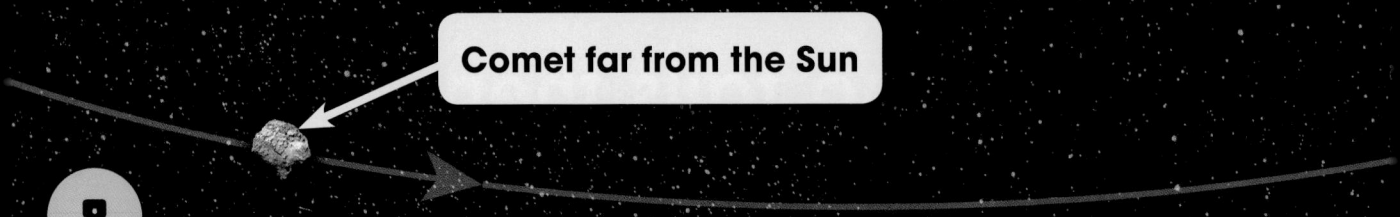

The gas and dust form tails.

Comets often have two tails.

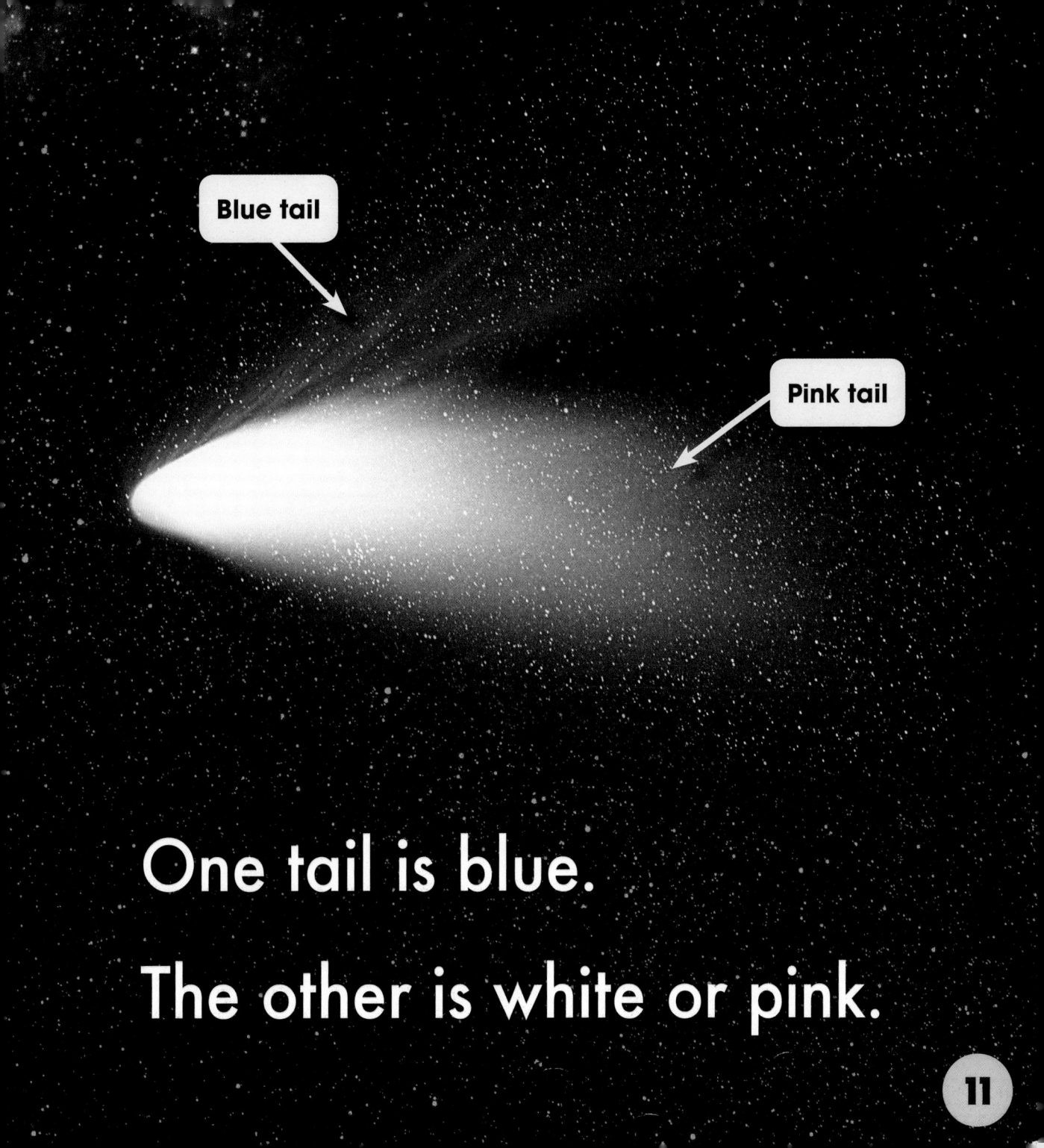

One tail is blue.

The other is white or pink.

The front of the comet is called the head.

Comet heads can be as big as mountains.

Comet tails are very long.

They can be more than 300 million miles (483 million km) long!

Our Solar System has many comets.

About 4,000 have been discovered.

A few comets come close enough to Earth for us to see.

Halley's Comet passes by our planet about every 76 years.

It will pass by Earth again in 2061.

Spacecraft have explored comets.

One spacecraft brought dust from a comet's tail back to Earth!

A spacecraft

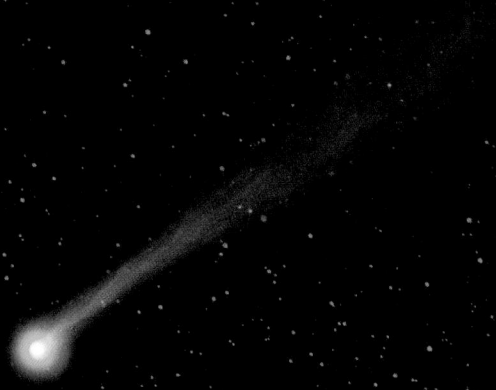

COMETS	VERSUS	EARTH
Orbit the Sun	PATH IN SPACE	Orbits the Sun
Solid head, up to 25 miles (40 km) across; Tail, up to 360 million miles (579,363,840 km) long	SIZE	7,918 miles (12,743 km) across
Frozen gases, rock, and dust	SURFACE	Mostly oceans, with some land

GLOSSARY

gases (GASS-iz) substances that float in the air and are neither liquid nor solid; many gases are invisible

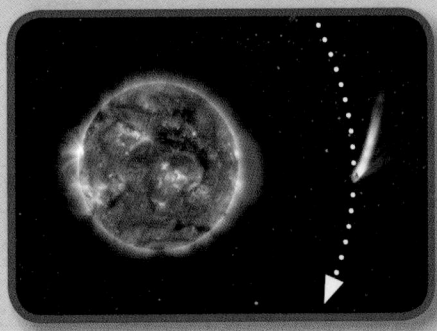

orbit (OR-bit) to circle around a planet, the Sun, or another object

Solar System (SOH-lur SISS-tuhm) the Sun and everything that circles around it, including the eight planets

spacecraft (SPAYSS-kraft) vehicles that can travel in space

INDEX

Earth 18–19, 20, 22
Halley's Comet 18–19
head 12–13, 22
size 13, 14–15, 22
Solar System 16
spacecraft 20–21
Sun 6–7, 8–9, 10, 22
tails 4–5, 7, 10–11, 14–15, 20, 22

READ MORE

Chrismer, Melanie. *Comets (Scholastic News Nonfiction Readers).* New York: Children's Press (2005).

Lawrence, Ellen. *Comets, Meteors, and Asteroids: Voyagers of the Solar System (Zoom Into Space).* New York: Ruby Tuesday Books (2014).

LEARN MORE ONLINE

To learn more about comets, visit
www.bearportpublishing.com/OutOfThisWorld

ABOUT THE AUTHOR

Chaya Glaser enjoys looking up at the stars and reading stories about the constellations. When she's not admiring the night sky, she can be found playing musical instruments.